THE CORRECT MINDSET TO START A HOME BASED BUSINESS

Asaf Iqbal

CONTENTS

CHAPTER 1:
INTRODUCTION

Amidst the rapidly advancing and constantly evolving world, traditional methods of achieving success just don't quite cut it anymore. With the rise of technology and the internet, the game has changed. The world is more connected than ever before, with a wealth of knowledge and resources available at our fingertips. A "go-getter" attitude and hard work are no longer enough to sustain success.

To achieve success in the current era, one must embrace a modern mindset. This means being open to change and constantly adapting to the ever-changing landscape of the business world. It means understanding the importance of technology and its role in enhancing our chances for success.

The digital era has also brought about a shift in the understanding of the definition of success. It can no longer be confined to the narrow definition of financial gain. Instead, success is now defined by a more holistic approach, encompassing personal growth, making a positive impact, and contributing to society.

In the age of technology, one must also recognise the importance of building relationships. Networking has never been easier with the vast reach of social media. However, the art of networking extends beyond just making connections online. Successful networkers must also master the art of meaningful conversations and know the right time to initiate them.

The science behind achieving success has been a point of interest for generations. New studies have shown that the habits and traits of highly successful people are grounded in psychology and neuroscience. Another takeaway is that embracing failure can provide valuable insights which, in turn, can make way for better opportunities.

Finally, one must not forget the importance of balancing work and life. The irony in today's fast-paced world is that slowing down can sometimes lead to speeding up.

Finding time for relaxation, exercise, and hobbies can work wonders for productivity as well as mental and emotional well-being.

The modern era of technology and the internet has brought about an entirely different definition of success and ways of achieving it. To make strides in today's world, one must be digital-savvy, receptive to change, and possess a holistic mindset. Only then can one achieve success that stands the test of time.

As we live in the age of advanced technology, we have the power to leverage it for our success. The availability of technology has made it possible for us to achieve our dreams in a more efficient and effective way. From smartphones to the internet, technology has changed the way we live, work, and interact with one another.

One of the ways technology can enhance our chances for success is by providing us with a vast amount of information. Thanks to the internet, we have access to nearly limitless knowledge. With just a few clicks, we can learn new skills, gain new insights, and connect with experts around the world. This information empowers us to make better decisions and take action towards our goals.

The internet also provides us with powerful communication tools that enable us to connect with people from all walks of life. Through social media platforms, we can build our personal brand and establish our online presence. This can lead to new opportunities such as partnerships, collaborations, and even job offers. Online networking has made business interactions faster and more convenient than ever before.

Another way technology can enhance our chances for success is through e-commerce. The rise of e-commerce has opened up new markets and opportunities for small business owners and entrepreneurs. Online marketplaces allow us to sell products and services to customers around the world. This can dramatically increase our potential customer base and lead to significant growth.

Moreover, the digital age has brought about a new future of work. Remote work arrangements and freelance opportunities have become increasingly popular. This means that location is no longer a barrier to success. We can work from anywhere and collaborate with people from any part of the world. This flexibility allows us to strike a balance between work and life.

Technology is a powerful tool that can help us achieve success in the modern era.
By leveraging the internet, e-commerce, and new forms of work arrangements, we can increase our chances of success. We must adapt to the changing times and learn how to use technology to our advantage. With the right mindset and tools, we can achieve greatness and live our best lives.

Developing a modern mindset for achieving success requires a shift in the way we think about success. In the digital age, success is not just about financial wealth, but rather a holistic definition that encompasses personal growth, social impact, and contribution to society. To develop this modern mindset, we must first let go of traditional notions of success that may hold us back.

One of the key principles of a modern mindset is adaptability. In the digital age, technology is constantly changing, and businesses must be able to keep up with these changes in order to succeed. Those who are able to adapt quickly and embrace new technologies will have a competitive advantage over those who resist change.

Another important aspect of a modern mindset is a focus on lifelong learning. In the digital age, information is readily available at our fingertips through the internet and online resources. It is important to continuously seek out new knowledge and skills to stay relevant and competitive in the modern workforce.

A modern mindset also requires a focus on collaboration and community building. In a world that is increasingly connected through technology, success often depends on our ability to build strong relationships and networks. By working together and leveraging each other's strengths, we can achieve greater success and make a positive impact on the world.

In order to develop a modern mindset for achieving success, it is important to be open to change, embrace lifelong learning, and focus on collaboration and building strong relationships. By adopting these principles, we can not only achieve financial success, but also find fulfilment in our personal and professional lives.

Success is a concept of life that has been constantly evolving over the years. It is not just about accumulating wealth, but also about achieving self-fulfilment and leaving a mark in the world. As the world advances and technology becomes ubiquitous, new opportunities for success arise, and new challenges to overcome.

In the past, success was often equated with financial wealth. People aimed to accumulate as much money and assets as possible, and this was seen as the ultimate goal of their lives. However, with the advent of the digital age, success has taken on a new definition. Today, success is not just about material wealth, but also about innovation, creativity, and social impact.

With the power of technology, individuals have greater control over their own success. They can leverage the internet to showcase their strengths, connect with like-minded individuals, and access resources that were previously unavailable. The rise of online learning and e-commerce has opened up new avenues for growth and prosperity. People no longer need to rely solely on traditional institutions or brick-and-mortar businesses to achieve their goals.

The mindset for success has also undergone a shift. In the past, success was often attributed to innate abilities or luck. However, today's successful individuals understand that hard work, perseverance, and resilience are essential components of a successful life. They acknowledge that failure is not a setback, but rather an opportunity for growth and learning.

As we progress further into the digital age, success will continue to evolve and take on new meanings. With the rise of artificial intelligence, the definition of success may once again change. However, one thing is clear: those who are willing to adapt to these changes and embrace the power of modern technology will be well-positioned to achieve success in the current era.

In today's fast-paced digital world, success is no longer confined to financial wealth. The modern definition of success encompasses a much broader range of aspirations and achievements. It includes finding purpose and fulfilment in one's work, building meaningful relationships, and making a positive impact on the world.

While financial wealth remains an important component of success, it is just one aspect of a much more comprehensive picture. Nowadays, people are more concerned about living a well-rounded life that also includes social and emotional wealth. This shift is not driven solely by millennials or the new generation; it's fast becoming a global phenomenon.

To achieve success beyond financial wealth requires focusing on personal growth, discovering one's purpose, and developing a mindset that priorities personal well-being and happiness. It involves learning to nurture relationships, exploring new opportunities, and cultivating resilience to overcome setbacks.

In today's interconnected world, success has become about making a positive impact on society. Whether it's through charitable contributions, political activism, or community volunteering, success now incorporates using one's talent and resources for the betterment of all.

As we move deeper into the digital age, the definition of success continues to evolve. In a world dominated by technology, success doesn't just mean overcoming financial obstacles; it's also about overcoming digital ones. It's about mastering new skills and harnessing the power of technology to our advantage.

Success is no longer just about financial wealth. The modern definition of success encompasses a whole range of aspirations and achievements, including personal growth, fulfilling relationships, making an impact on society, and using technology to our advantage. It's an exciting era to be alive, and those who embrace its power will be the ones to succeed in this new era.

CHAPTER 2: THE POWER OF THE INTERNET

In today's world, businesses can't afford to overlook the internet as a tool for success. From e-commerce to online marketing and customer engagement, the internet has revolutionised the way businesses operate.

First and foremost, having a strong online presence is crucial for any business. This means having a user-friendly website that provides valuable content and easy navigation. The website should also be optimised for search engine rankings, so customers can easily find what they're looking for.

Social media platforms should also be a key component of any business's online strategy. By creating engaging content and leveraging advanced targeting features, businesses can reach their desired audience with precision. Social media also provides an opportunity for authentic customer engagement and feedback.

Another way to leverage the internet for success is through online learning and training. Whether it's through webinars, online courses, or workshops, businesses can stay up-to-date with the latest trends and technologies in their industry.

Lastly, e-commerce has exploded in recent years, providing businesses with a new and lucrative avenue to increase sales. By creating user-friendly online stores and leveraging the power of online marketplaces, businesses can exponentially increase their reach and sales potential.

Overall, the internet provides countless opportunities for businesses to succeed in the digital age. By embracing these strategies and staying up-to-date with the latest technologies, businesses can thrive in an ever-evolving market.

In today's digital age, social media has become an incredibly powerful and effective tool for personal branding and success. With billions of people active on social media platforms such as Facebook, Instagram, Twitter, LinkedIn, and others, the potential for connecting with others and building a personal brand has never been greater.

One of the key benefits of social media is its ability to help individuals and businesses reach a large audience quickly and easily. By creating valuable and engaging content that resonates with your target audience, social media platforms can help you build your reputation and establish yourself as an authority in your field. This can lead to increased visibility, new business opportunities, and an expanded network of contacts.

In addition to building your reputation and personal brand, social media can also provide valuable insights into your target audience. By monitoring trends and analysing metrics such as engagement rates, click-through rates, and conversion rates, you can gain a better understanding of what resonates with your audience and tailor your content and messaging accordingly.

Of course, social media also has its challenges. With so much content being created and shared every day, it can be difficult to stand out from the crowd. It's important to be strategic with your social media efforts, focusing on creating high-quality content that adds value to your audience and supports your overall goals.

Another challenge of social media is the need to balance personal and professional branding. While social media can be a powerful tool for building your personal brand and establishing yourself as an authority in your field, it's important to remember that what you post online can also have a significant impact on your personal and professional reputation.

In order to successfully leverage social media for personal branding and success, it's critical to develop a clear strategy and focus on creating high-quality, valuable content that resonates with your target audience. Whether you're an entrepreneur, freelancer, or working professional, social media can be a powerful tool for building your reputation, expanding your network, and achieving success in the modern digital age.

Another benefit of today's digital world, the internet has revolutionised the way we learn. Online learning has opened up a world of opportunities for those looking to enhance their skills and knowledge in a particular area. The rise of Massive Open Online Courses (MOOCs) has given people from all corners of the world access to top-quality educational resources from leading universities and institutions.

The convenience and flexibility of online learning are unparalleled. Students can learn at their own pace, from anywhere in the world, without having to worry about commuting or fitting classes into their busy schedules. This means that people who may not have had access to traditional educational opportunities can now pursue their dreams and expand their knowledge base.

Online learning is not limited to just academic courses either. There are numerous online resources available for developing skills such as coding, graphic design, or even writing. Companies like LinkedIn Learning and Udemy offer a wide range of courses on various subjects, tailored to individuals' needs and interests.

Online learning can enhance one's career prospects. According to a study by the Babson Survey Research Group, 74% of surveyed academic leaders believed that learning outcomes from online education are equal to or better than traditional classroom-based learning. This means that pursuing an online course can help you gain new skills and knowledge that you can showcase to potential employers, making you a more attractive candidate in the job market.

Online learning is a powerful tool that can help individuals enhance their chances of success in today's digital age. By leveraging the vast resources available online, individuals can expand their knowledge base, acquire new skills, and improve their career prospects.

Embracing the power of online learning is a game-changer for anyone looking to achieve their goals in the 21st century.

In today's world, e-commerce has emerged as a major player in the modern economy. With the rise of online shopping and platforms such as Amazon, Alibaba and eBay, e-commerce has become an essential part of the business landscape.

One of the key benefits of e-commerce is its ability to easily reach a global audience. Businesses can sell their products and services to anyone, anywhere in the world. This opens up new markets and customers that were previously inaccessible, allowing businesses to expand in ways never before possible.

Another advantage of e-commerce is the ability to collect and analyse data about consumers. Online retailers can track customer behaviour and preferences, allowing them to make more informed decisions about product offerings, pricing, and marketing strategies.

E-commerce also offers a level of convenience that traditional brick-and-mortar stores cannot match. Customers can shop from the comfort of their own homes, avoiding crowds, traffic, and long lines. As a result, online shopping has become increasingly popular, especially among millennials.

However, e-commerce also presents its own set of challenges. Competition is fierce in the online marketplace, with thousands of businesses vying for attention and sales. Customers have high expectations when it comes to the quality of products and services, and negative online reviews can quickly damage a business's reputation.

Therefore, it is crucial for businesses to not only leverage the benefits of e-commerce, but also to carefully navigate its challenges. As the economy continues to evolve, e-commerce will undoubtedly play an even greater role in the success of businesses both large and small.

In the digital age, the future of work is rapidly evolving. With the advent of new technologies and the internet, the traditional workplace is dramatically changing. As more and more people around the world have access to the internet, the opportunities for remote work and telecommuting are increasing. Today, the concept of a traditional nine-to-five workday is becoming increasingly outdated.

In a digital world, work is no longer defined by the setting in which it is performed. Work can be done from anywhere, at any time. This has led to the rise of the gig economy, where workers are increasingly seeking out short-term, contract-based work rather than traditional, long-term employment.
With the increasing prevalence of online platforms and marketplaces, freelancers can now connect with clients from all over the world, allowing them to take on a variety of projects that suit their skillsets.

At the same time, the digital age has also created new industries and job categories that never existed before. For example, the rise of artificial intelligence and machine learning has led to the creation of many specialised roles in this field, such as data scientists and machine learning engineers. Similarly, the growth of e-commerce has led to a surge in demand for specialists in logistics and supply chain management.

In this changing landscape, it is increasingly important for individuals to be flexible and adaptable. Workers who can quickly learn and master new skills are likely to be the most successful in the digital age. Employers are seeking out candidates who can offer a diverse skillset, and are willing to invest in training and education to help their employees stay up-to-date with the latest trends and technologies.

The future of work in a digital world is exciting, but also challenging. The internet and new technologies are changing the way we work, and it is up to individuals, companies, and governments to adapt to these changes and create a sustainable and rewarding future for all. With the right mindset, skills, and training, anyone can succeed in the digital age.

CHAPTER 3: THE RISE OF ARTIFICIAL INTELLIGENCE

Understanding the Basics of Artificial Intelligence:

In order to fully grasp the potential that Artificial Intelligence (AI) holds for success in the modern era, it is crucial to first understand what AI is and how it works.

At its core, AI refers to the development of computer systems that can perform tasks that normally require human intervention such as learning, reasoning, and decision-making. Simply put, AI is the practice of training computers to think and act like humans. AI systems work by utilising a variety of technologies and techniques such as neural networks, natural language processing, and computer vision. These tools allow computers to analyse vast amounts of data and make decisions based on that analysis.

One of the most promising applications of AI is in the field of automation. By automating repetitive and mundane tasks, businesses can save time and resources while also increasing productivity. Additionally, AI can be used to analyse data and identify patterns and trends that may not be immediately apparent to humans.

While the potential of AI is immense, it is not without its risks. The increasing reliance on AI systems can raise concerns around job loss, biases, and the ethical implications of decision-making performed by machines.

Overall, understanding the basics of AI is essential for anyone looking to leverage this technology for success. As AI continues to evolve and become more sophisticated, individuals and businesses must remain informed and adapt in order to unlock its full potential while mitigating any potential risks.

In today's world, technology is playing a crucial role in how businesses operate and achieve success. One of the most significant advancements in technology that is changing the game for businesses is Artificial Intelligence (AI). AI has the potential to transform the way businesses operate by automating various processes, providing real-time insights, and enhancing decision-making capabilities.

In the current era, businesses have access to an immense amount of data, which can be overwhelming to analyse manually. AI algorithms can process this data at a much faster rate and provide insights that can help businesses make informed decisions. AI can also help businesses automate and streamline various processes, reducing human error and costs.

For example, AI-powered chatbots can help businesses provide 24/7 customer support, reducing the need for human customer support representatives. AI algorithms can also optimise supply chain management, reducing costs and increasing efficiency. In addition, AI can help businesses analyse market trends and customer behaviour patterns, enabling them to make strategic decisions and stay ahead of the competition.

However, with the benefits of AI come ethical concerns. The potential impact of AI on employment, privacy, and security must be considered. There is a need for businesses to ensure that AI is being deployed ethically and responsibly.

In conclusion, AI is transforming the way businesses operate by providing real-time insights, automating processes, and enhancing decision-making capabilities. However, ethical concerns surrounding AI must be addressed to ensure that the potential benefits of AI are not outweighed by the costs. Businesses must embrace AI while being mindful of its ethical implications to achieve success in today's digital age.

Artificial Intelligence (AI) has become a hot topic in recent years, with many experts predicting that it will revolutionise the way we live and work. While there are certainly many potential benefits to AI, there are also some significant risks that must be considered.

One of the most significant benefits of AI is its ability to automate tasks that are currently done by humans. This can lead to greater efficiency and productivity, as well as cost savings for businesses. For example, AI can be used to analyse large amounts of data much more quickly and accurately than humans, allowing companies to make better-informed decisions.

AI can also improve safety and security in a variety of industries. For example, self-driving cars are being developed that can potentially reduce the number of accidents caused by human error. AI can also be used for security purposes, such as monitoring surveillance footage for suspicious activity.

However, there are also significant risks associated with AI.

One of the biggest concerns is the potential for job loss as AI and automation replace human workers. This could lead to a significant increase in unemployment and could exacerbate income inequality.

Another concern is the potential misuse of AI, particularly by governments or other powerful entities. For example, AI could be used to create highly realistic fake news or propaganda, which could be used to manipulate public opinion or even incite violence.

There is the risk of AI becoming too powerful and potentially harmful. Some experts have raised concerns about the possibility of AI becoming uncontrollable or even turning against its creators. This could have catastrophic consequences for society and the economy.

Despite these risks, the potential benefits of AI cannot be ignored. As we continue to develop and deploy AI, it is important that we take steps to mitigate these risks and ensure that the technology is used in a responsible and ethical manner. By doing so, we can harness the power of AI to create a more prosperous and equitable society.

In today's digital age, artificial intelligence is transforming the way businesses operate and individuals achieve success. With the potential to streamline processes, reduce costs, and improve efficiency, AI has become a game-changer for those who know how to leverage it.

For businesses, AI can provide valuable insights and analytics for decision-making, automate mundane tasks, and even personalise customer experiences. From chatbots to predictive analytics, the possibilities for AI in business are endless. However, it's important to note that AI should not replace human skills and judgement. Rather, it should augment them and allow businesses to focus on higher-level thinking and problem-solving.

On an individual level, AI can enhance productivity and help people make smarter decisions. For example, by using AI-powered virtual assistants or calendar apps, individuals can manage their time more effectively and stay organised. Additionally, AI can provide personalised recommendations for products or services based on an individual's preferences and previous behaviour.

But as with any new technology, there are also risks and ethical implications to consider. It's important to ensure that AI is being used ethically and transparently, and that privacy and security concerns are addressed.

Ultimately, the key to leveraging AI for success is to stay informed and adapt to new technologies as they emerge. By embracing AI and incorporating it into our business and personal strategies, we can position ourselves for success in today's digital age.

As we continue to embrace artificial intelligence (AI) in our daily lives and in business, it's important to consider the ethical implications of this rapidly advancing technology. Many people are concerned about the possibility of AI replacing human jobs, biased decision-making, and even the potential for AI to become more intelligent than humans and pose a threat to humanity.

However, it's important to note that AI itself is not inherently good or bad. It's the way we design, develop, and use AI that determines whether it has a positive or negative impact on society. As such, it's critical that we prioritise ethical considerations when it comes to AI development and deployment. One important step towards ensuring ethical AI is to promote transparency and accountability in its development and use. This means ensuring that the algorithms and data used to train AI systems are unbiased and free from discrimination. It also means providing clear explanations for how AI systems make decisions, so that humans can understand and potentially challenge those decisions if necessary.

Another important ethical consideration is the potential impact of AI on the job market and society as a whole. While AI has the potential to create jobs and enhance productivity, it's also likely to automate many jobs that are currently performed by humans. This may lead to significant job losses and potentially widening economic inequality. As such, it's important to consider ways to support workers who may be displaced by AI, such as retraining programs and social safety nets.

Ultimately, ensuring the ethical development and use of AI requires collaboration and cooperation among stakeholders. This includes government regulators, AI developers, businesses, and society as a whole. By working together, we can harness the power of AI to enhance our lives and achieve success while ensuring that its impact is positive and beneficial for everyone.

CHAPTER 4: THE IMPORTANCE OF NETWORKING

In today's digital age, networking has never been more crucial for achieving success. With
the rise of technology and the internet, individuals and businesses alike have a vast array
of tools at their disposal to build and maintain a strong network of contacts.

Networking in the modern world goes beyond traditional face-to-face interactions. Social media platforms such as LinkedIn, Twitter, and Instagram provide individuals with the opportunity to connect with others on a global scale. Online networking also allows individuals to overcome geographical limitations and build relationships with like-minded individuals in different parts of the world.

Successful networking in the digital age requires a strategic approach. It's essential to identify and target individuals or groups that align with your goals and interests. Creating and sharing valuable content on social media platforms can also help to showcase your expertise and attract like-minded individuals.

However, it's important to remember that networking in the modern world is not just about self-promotion. A strong network is built on mutual relationships and adding value to others. By offering support, advice, and mentorship to others, you'll not only build genuine relationships but also open up new opportunities for yourself.

In today's digital age, networking remains a crucial element for achieving success. By utilising the power of technology and adopting a strategic approach, individuals and businesses can build and maintain a strong network of contacts that can provide valuable support and opportunities.

Building and maintaining a strong network online is imperative in today's digital age. Whether you are an entrepreneur, a job seeker, or a professional seeking to stay ahead in your field, having a strong network of connections can make all the difference in achieving your goals. Here are some tips for building and maintaining a strong online network:

1. Start with LinkedIn: LinkedIn is the go-to platform for professional networking online. It's where you can connect with colleagues, friends, and industry leaders. Make sure your LinkedIn profile is updated and professional-looking. Also, don't forget to customise your LinkedIn URL to make it easy for people to find you.

2. Participate in Online Communities: Find online communities in your industry or area of interest and participate in discussions. Share your thoughts, expertise, and insights. This is a great way to build relationships with people who share your interests.

3. Attend Virtual Networking Events: Many organisations are hosting virtual events these days. Attend as many as you can, and introduce yourself to others. These events are a great opportunity to connect with people in your industry and beyond.

4. Engage on Social Media: Social media platforms like Twitter, Instagram, and Facebook can be great tools for networking if used correctly. Engage with people by commenting on their posts,

sharing their content, and responding to their messages. This is a great way to build relationships with people outside of your immediate circle.

5. Follow Up: After meeting someone new online, make sure to follow up with them. Send them a message or an email to thank them for connecting with you. Keeping in touch and maintaining relationships is crucial for long-term success.

Building a strong network takes time, effort, and persistence. Focus on building real relationships and adding value to others, and success will naturally follow.

In today's digital age, social media has become a crucial tool for building meaningful connections and growing one's network. While it may seem daunting at first, leveraging social media for building relationships is easier than it seems.

Firstly, it's important to identify the platforms that align with your personal and professional goals. LinkedIn, for example, is a great platform for professional networking while Instagram could be more useful for creative individuals.

Once you have identified the platforms, start by optimising your profiles. Make sure your online presence represents your personal brand and showcases your skills and expertise. Share relevant content and engage with others by commenting on their posts or sending personalised messages.

Joining relevant groups or communities can also expand your network. This could be groups related to your industry or interests and can provide opportunities for building relationships with like-minded individuals.

Remember that building real relationships takes time and effort. Consistent engagement and follow-ups are key to maintaining relationships and building trust.

With the right strategies, social media can be a powerful tool for building meaningful connections and growing a strong network that can lead to future opportunities for success.

Crafting Effective Cold Emails for Success:

In the digital age, cold emailing has become an essential tool for building new relationships and expanding networks. However, with emails flooding our inboxes every day, it is becoming increasingly difficult to stand out from the crowd. To master the art of crafting effective cold emails, there are several key strategies that can be implemented.

First and foremost, understanding the recipient's perspective is crucial. Instead of simply pitching your product or service, focus on providing value to the recipient. Research their interests, company, and pain points, and tailor your email accordingly. This will not only grab their attention, but also establish trust and credibility.

Another important element of effective cold emailing is personalisation. Use the recipient's name in the greeting, and reference previous conversations or mutual connections if applicable. This shows that you have taken the time to research and personalise the email, and increases the chances of a response.

In addition, the subject line is a crucial component of any cold email. It should be short, attention-grabbing, and relevant to the recipient's interests or pain points. Avoid using overly sales-y language or irrelevant information.

Furthermore, the body of the email should be concise and compelling. Use a conversational tone, and focus on the recipient's needs and interests. Provide specific examples of how your product or service can help them overcome their challenges or achieve their goals.

Finally, always include a clear call to action in the email. This could be a request for a meeting, a phone call, or simply a reply to the email. Make it easy for the recipient to take the desired action, and provide any necessary next steps or information.

Mastering the art of crafting effective cold emails takes practice and patience. By focusing on providing value, personalisation, and clear calls to action, you can increase the chances of building meaningful connections and expanding your network.

As an introvert, building a strong network can be challenging, but it is not impossible. Here are some tips to help you build meaningful connections despite your reserved nature.

Firstly, identify your strengths and interests to find common ground with potential connections. Join groups or attend events related to your passions, as this will make it easier to strike up conversations and form genuine connections.

Secondly, take advantage of online networking tools such as LinkedIn or Twitter. These platforms allow you to connect with like-minded individuals and professionals in your industry. You can engage in conversation without the pressure of face-to-face interaction, making it easier to build relationships.

Thirdly, embrace the power of one-on-one interactions. Introverts often excel in smaller, more intimate settings, so try setting up coffee meetings or phone calls with people you admire or would like to learn from.
Finally, don't be afraid to embrace your introverted nature. Rather than trying to force yourself to be outgoing, focus on building deeper, more meaningful relationships with a select few individuals.

Remember, networking is not just about meeting people, it's about building relationships. By playing to your strengths as an introvert and being intentional about forming genuine connections, you can build a strong network that will contribute to your success.

CHAPTER 5: THE SCIENCE OF SUCCESS

Success is not just a matter of luck or talent, it's also about having the right mindset.

Successful people have a particular way of thinking that sets them apart from the rest. Understanding the psychology behind successful people can provide valuable insights into what it takes to achieve success in the current era.

One of the core traits of successful people is a growth mindset. This means that they see challenges as opportunities to learn and grow, rather than obstacles to be overcome. They embrace failure as part of the learning process and are not afraid to take risks or try new things. They also have a strong sense of self-belief and resilience which enables them to persevere in the face of adversity.

Successful people also have a clear vision of what they want to achieve. They set goals that are specific, measurable, achievable, relevant and time-bound. They break down their goals into smaller actionable steps and focus on what they can do in the present moment to move closer to their desired outcome.

Another key trait of successful people is their ability to manage their emotions and stay focused on the task at hand. They have a high degree of self-awareness and can recognise their own emotional states. They also have the ability to regulate their emotions and maintain a positive mindset even in the face of setbacks and challenges.

Successful people also have strong interpersonal skills. They are able to communicate effectively, build relationships, and work collaboratively with others. They are receptive to feedback and are always looking for ways to improve themselves and their work.

Finally, successful people have a strong work ethic and are willing to put in the time and effort necessary to achieve their goals. They are disciplined and organised, and have a clear sense of priorities. They also understand the importance of maintaining a healthy work-life balance and taking care of their physical and mental well-being.

Overall, understanding the psychology behind successful people provides valuable insights into what it takes to achieve success in the current era. Developing a growth mindset, setting clear goals, managing emotions, developing strong interpersonal skills, and maintaining a strong work ethic are all key factors in achieving success in today's world.

Examining the commonalities among successful individuals begins with understanding that success is not just a product of one's talents or abilities. Rather, successful individuals possess certain traits and habits that contribute to their achievements. These traits include resilience, perseverance, creativity, adaptability, discipline, focus, and goal-setting skills.

Furthermore, successful individuals have a growth mindset, which means they are open to learning and growth. They view challenges as opportunities to learn and improve rather than obstacles to be avoided. Additionally, successful individuals surround themselves with supportive and positive people who encourage and inspire them to reach their goals.

In terms of habits, successful individuals often have a strong work ethic and are dedicated to their craft. They prioritise their time and use it wisely, often employing effective time management techniques. They also prioritise their health and well-being, maintaining good physical and mental health through exercise, proper nutrition, and self-care practices.

Successful individuals have a clear vision of their goals and work diligently towards achieving them. They are persistent in the face of setbacks and failures, using them as opportunities to learn and improve. Throughout their journey to success, they remain focused and committed to their goals, constantly striving towards excellence.

Examining the commonalities among successful individuals reveals that success is not solely determined by one's innate talents or abilities. Rather, success is the result of a combination of traits, habits, and mindset, coupled with hard work, discipline, and a clear vision of one's goals. By developing these key attributes, anyone can increase their chances of achieving success in their chosen field.

Failures as Stepping Stones to Success:
Mistakes and failures are inevitable parts of life, especially when striving for success. However, instead of fearing failure, successful individuals embrace and learn from their failures. In fact, many successful people attribute their achievements to the lessons they learned from their past failures.
One key aspect of turning failures into stepping stones to success is to adopt a growth mindset. This means embracing challenges as opportunities to learn and improve, rather than letting setbacks define one's abilities or self-worth. By viewing failures as a chance to grow and evolve, individuals can bounce back stronger and more resilient than before.

Another way to turn failures into opportunities for growth is to embrace the power of feedback. Constructive feedback from others can highlight areas that need improvement and provide valuable insights for future success. Rather than shying away from criticism, successful individuals seek out feedback and use it to improve their skills and performance.

It's important to remember that failures do not define one's worth or future success. Instead, failures should be viewed as a necessary and valuable part of the journey to achieving success. With the right mindset and approach, failures can serve as important stepping stones towards achieving one's goals and dreams.

Exploring the neuroscience behind what makes people successful takes us into the world of brain science. Recent research has revealed that regions of the brain linked with learning and memory, particularly the prefrontal cortex and the hippocampus, play a crucial role in determining one's capacity for success.

The prefrontal cortex, which is responsible for decision-making, problem-solving, and reasoning, has been found to be more active in individuals who are successful. Furthermore, the size of this region has been found to correlate positively with success, as individuals with larger prefrontal cortices are thought to have a greater capacity for learning, making complex decisions, and working towards long-term goals.

Another region of the brain linked with success is the hippocampus, which is involved in memory consolidation and spatial awareness. This region has been shown to be more active in individuals with strong problem-solving skills and a capacity for creative thinking.

In addition to these brain regions, studies have revealed the importance of neuroplasticity in achieving success. Neuroplasticity refers to the ability of the brain to adapt, change and develop new neural connections in response to new experiences. This means that individuals who commit to learning and consistently challenging their brains are more likely to develop new neural pathways, allowing them to better navigate complex situations and make more informed decisions.

Research has revealed that practicing mindfulness and incorporating meditation into one's daily routine can influence the structure and function of the brain in ways that are conducive to success. Mindfulness practices have been shown to increase cortical thickness, improve memory, increase focus and attention, and reduce stress levels, which are all critical for achieving success in any context.

Overall, exploring the neuroscience behind success has revealed that the key to success lies not only in our abilities and hard work but also in the structure and function of our brains. By understanding how our brains work and actively working to improve them through mindfulness, neuroplasticity, and consistent learning, we can unlock our full potential for success in a complex and ever-changing world.

Mindfulness practices have gained significant attention in recent years for their potential to improve overall wellbeing and, in turn, enhance success. Mindfulness can be defined as the practice of being present in the moment and non-judgmentally aware of one's thoughts and surroundings. When applied to achieving success, mindfulness can help individuals to focus on their goals and enhance their ability to manage stress and distractions.

One of the key benefits of mindfulness is its ability to strengthen areas of the brain that are associated with attention, focus, and decision-making. As individuals practice mindfulness, they learn to control their attention and maintain focus on the task at hand, which can be crucial for achieving success in a constantly distracted world.

In addition to improving focus and attention, mindfulness practices have also been proven to reduce stress levels, which can be a significant barrier to success. High levels of stress can negatively impact decision-making and overall productivity, but with mindfulness, individuals can learn to manage stress more effectively.

Mindfulness practices can range from simple breathing exercises to more structured meditations. The key is to find a practice that works for each individual and incorporate it into their daily routine. By practicing mindfulness regularly, individuals can improve their ability to focus, manage stress, and ultimately achieve greater success in all areas of their lives.

CHAPTER 6: THE ART OF PRODUCTIVITY

In today's fast-paced world, effective time management is essential for achieving success. It's not just about getting more done in less time, but also making sure that the time spent is focused on the most important tasks that bring us closer to our goals. The key to effective time management is prioritisation and planning.

We often feel overwhelmed with the number of tasks we have to do, but by dividing them into smaller, manageable chunks, we can make progress without feeling bogged down. One popular method is the Pomodoro Technique, where we work for 25-minute intervals followed by short breaks. This allows us to stay focused on a specific task and take breaks when needed, ultimately boosting productivity.

However, time management isn't just about fitting as many tasks as possible into a day. It's also crucial to schedule time for rest, relaxation, and self-care. Without a proper work-life balance, burnout can occur, which ultimately hinders productivity and success.

To maximise productivity, it's also crucial to eliminate distractions as much as possible. Turning off notifications on our smartphones and limiting social media use during work hours can help us stay focused on our tasks.

By implementing effective time management strategies and prioritising self-care, we can boost productivity, achieve our goals, and live a more fulfilling life. Time is a valuable resource, and how we choose to spend it can make all the difference in our success.

Boosting productivity is a crucial aspect of achieving success in today's fast-paced world. With so many distractions and demands on our time, it's easy to lose sight of our goals and fail to accomplish what we set out to do. That's where effective time management techniques come in.

One popular method for boosting productivity is the Pomodoro Technique. This technique involves breaking your workday into 25-minute intervals, or "pomodoros," followed by short breaks. The idea is to work intensely for a short period of time, and then take a break to recharge before starting the next pomodoro.

By using the Pomodoro Technique, you can avoid burnout and maintain your focus throughout the day. The regular breaks also help to prevent procrastination and keep you motivated. Additionally, the structure of the Pomodoro Technique can help you to prioritise your tasks and make progress toward your goals.

To get started with the Pomodoro Technique, set a timer for 25 minutes and work on a task without any distractions. Once the timer goes off, take a short break for 5-10 minutes before starting the next pomodoro. After completing four pomodoros, take a longer break of 20-30 minutes to recharge.

The Pomodoro Technique is a simple yet effective way to boost productivity and achieve success in the modern era. By incorporating this technique into your daily routine, you can make the most of your time and reach your full potential.

In a world where smartphones, social media, and other digital distractions are constantly vying for our attention, maintaining focus and staying productive can be a challenge.

Another way to stay focused is to prioritise tasks and create a to-do list. This can help you stay organised and focused on the most important tasks, without getting sidetracked by less important activities.

Finally, taking care of your physical and mental health can also help you stay focused and productive. This includes getting enough sleep, exercising regularly, and taking breaks throughout the day to stretch or practice mindfulness meditation.

By implementing these strategies, you can stay focused and productive in a world full of distractions, helping you achieve success in both your personal and professional life.

Maximising productivity for success is not just about getting things done; it's also about taking care of your physical and mental health. Exercise, sleep, and nutrition are three critical factors that can greatly enhance your chances for success.

First and foremost, exercise is essential for maintaining a healthy body and mind. Regular physical activity can reduce stress, increase productivity, and improve overall well-being. It can also boost energy levels, making it easier to tackle tasks throughout the day.

Sleep is equally important when it comes to productivity and success. Getting enough quality sleep is crucial for maintaining focus, memory, and cognitive function. Sleep deprivation, on the other hand, can lead to decreased productivity, increased errors, and a variety of health issues.

Nutrition plays a vital role in both physical and mental health. Eating a well-balanced diet that's rich in nutrients can improve concentration, memory, and creativity. It can also provide the energy needed to power through busy schedules and stay focused on tasks at hand.

Incorporating exercise, sleep, and nutrition into your daily routine may seem daunting, but small changes can lead to significant improvements. Set realistic goals and make gradual changes to your habits. Take breaks to stretch or go for a walk during the day, prioritise a consistent sleep schedule, and opt for nutritious snacks instead of junk food.

By prioritising your physical and mental health, you'll not only increase your chances for success but also enjoy the journey along the way. Remember, success isn't just about what you achieve, but also how you achieve it.

Maintaining a healthy work-life balance is crucial for achieving success in the digital age. With technology advancing rapidly and businesses becoming more competitive, it's easy to get caught up in work and neglect other areas of our lives. However, research has shown that those who maintain a healthy work-life balance have greater productivity, higher job satisfaction, and overall better well-being.

One way to achieve a healthy work-life balance is by setting clear boundaries and priorities. It's important to establish specific work hours and stick to them, as well as prioritise important tasks and delegate or eliminate tasks that are less important. Additionally, it's important to give ourselves time for rest and self-care, whether that means engaging in physical activity, practicing mindfulness, or simply spending time with loved ones.

In a world where we are constantly connected through technology, it's also crucial to set boundaries for our personal time. This could mean turning off notifications during certain hours of the day or designating certain days of the week as technology-free. By disconnecting from technology and allowing ourselves time to recharge, we can improve our mental and emotional well-being and ultimately increase our productivity and success.

Overall, maintaining a healthy work-life balance is not only important for our well-being but also for achieving success in the digital age. By setting clear boundaries, establishing priorities, and giving ourselves time for rest and self-care, we can optimise our productivity and achieve success in all areas of our lives.

CHAPTER 7: THE POWER OF CREATIVITY

Creativity is the ability to come up with new ideas, solutions, and approaches to problems. Whether it's in business or personal life, creativity can help individuals achieve success and stand out from the rest. But what exactly is creative thinking, and how can we develop this skill?

Creative thinking is the ability to think outside of the box, to question assumptions and explore new possibilities. It involves using imagination and intuition to generate fresh ideas and concepts. Creative thinking is often associated with artists, writers, and musicians, but it's a skill that can benefit anyone in any field.

Research has shown that there are different types of creative thinking. One of them is divergent thinking, which involves generating a wide variety of ideas, possibilities, and solutions. Convergent thinking, on the other hand, involves focusing on a single idea, solution, or concept and refining it. Both types of thinking are valuable, and the key is knowing when to use each one.

So how can we develop our creative thinking skills? One way is to expose ourselves to new and diverse experiences. Travel, learn a new language, or take up a new hobby. These kinds of experiences can help break us out of our usual thought patterns and inspire new ideas. It's also important to allow ourselves time for reflection and daydreaming. Giving our minds a break from constant stimulation can help us generate new connections and insights.

Another way to develop our creative thinking is to practice brainstorming. This involves generating a list of ideas without judgment or criticism. Group brainstorming sessions can also be effective, as they encourage collaboration and build off each other's ideas.

It's important to embrace failure as a necessary step in the creative process. Many successful creative individuals have experienced failure and setbacks along the way. Rather than seeing failure as a roadblock, they used it as an opportunity to learn and grow.

In today's fast-paced, constantly changing world, creative thinking skills are more important than ever. By understanding the science behind creative thinking and by practicing techniques to develop this skill, individuals can harness creativity for success in all areas of their lives.

In today's fast-paced business environment, creativity has become a key driver of success. Companies that are willing to innovate and think outside the box are the ones that are able to survive and thrive in this competitive landscape.

One of the ways in which creativity can enhance business success is through the development of new and innovative products and services. By encouraging employees to think creatively, companies are able to come up with fresh ideas that can help them differentiate themselves from the competition. This can lead to increased sales and market share, as well as a stronger brand reputation.

Creativity can also play a role in marketing and branding efforts. Companies that are able to create memorable and impactful advertising campaigns are more likely to capture the attention of consumers and build brand loyalty. Additionally, creative branding can help businesses stand out in a crowded marketplace and establish a unique identity that resonates with customers.

In addition to product development and marketing, creativity can also be instrumental in problem-solving and decision-making. Often, the most effective solutions to complex business challenges require fresh thinking and outside-the-box ideas. By fostering a culture of creativity, businesses can tap into the innovative ideas that exist within their own ranks and generate new solutions to longstanding problems.

Creativity can contribute to the overall culture of a company, creating an environment that is engaging, inspiring, and conducive to growth. By valuing and rewarding creativity, companies can attract and retain talented individuals who bring unique perspectives and a fresh approach to their work.

Creativity has become an essential ingredient in modern business success. By cultivating a culture of creativity, businesses can drive innovation and differentiate themselves from the competition, as well as solving complex problems and creating a thriving work environment.

Throughout history, creative thinkers have disrupted and transformed entire industries. One notable example is Elon Musk, whose innovative thinking and creativity have resulted in game-changing companies such as Tesla and SpaceX. His vision and endless pursuit of finding new ways to revolutionise industries have led to the development of electric cars, reusable rockets, and the potential for space exploration and colonisation.

Another inspiring example is the fashion brand, Zara, which disrupted the retail industry through a unique and innovative business model. Zara's fast-fashion approach involved producing smaller batches of clothing and continuously updating its inventory based on the latest trends. This business model enabled the company to respond quickly to changing fashion trends and customer demands, which resulted in increased sales and a loyal customer base.

Similarly, Airbnb revolutionised the lodging industry by offering a platform for homeowners to rent their homes or apartments to travellers. The company's unique concept disrupted the traditional hotel industry by providing customers with a more personalised and authentic travel experience. Airbnb's innovative approach has empowered millions of homeowners to become hospitality providers, while also providing travellers with affordable and unique accommodation options.

These examples demonstrate the power of creativity in disrupting industries and achieving success. By thinking outside of the box and challenging traditional business models, individuals and businesses can tap into new markets and create innovative solutions that cater to the needs of modern consumers. As the world continues to evolve, the ability to think creatively and adapt to change will be increasingly essential for achieving success in the digital age.

In the digital age, it's easy to get caught up in work and forget to make time for creative hobbies. However, embracing creativity and pursuing creative hobbies can actually enhance our chances for success. Engaging in creative activities provides numerous benefits, such as reducing stress, improving mental health and stimulating the brain.
Creative hobbies also help us develop new skills that can be applied to our work and boost productivity. For example, learning to play a musical instrument can improve hand-eye coordination, while practicing photography can enhance our attention to detail and creativity. Engaging in creative activities allows us to think outside the box and come up with innovative solutions to problems we may encounter in our work.

Furthermore, creative hobbies can serve as an outlet for passion and purpose, increasing our motivation and drive to succeed. Pursuing interests outside of work can provide a sense of fulfilment and happiness, which can spill over into other areas of our lives.

In today's competitive world, it's important to differentiate ourselves and stand out from the crowd. Adding creative hobbies to our repertoire can be a unique factor that sets us apart and makes us more memorable. It can also be a conversation starter and an opportunity to network with others who share similar interests.

The power of creativity should not be underestimated in regards to achieving success in the modern world. By embracing creative hobbies, we can enhance our chances for success by reducing stress, boosting productivity, developing new skills, finding purpose and standing out in the crowd.

Collaborating with others can be a powerful way to unlock creativity and find new solutions to the challenges we face. In the digital age, collaborating has become easier than ever, thanks to communication technologies that allow us to connect with people from all over the world.

One effective way to collaborate creatively is to join or form a mastermind group. Mastermind groups are made up of individuals with diverse skills, knowledge, and experience who come together to share ideas, offer feedback, and hold each other accountable for achieving their goals.
Joining a mastermind group can help you to find support, encouragement, and valuable insights from people who share your goals and challenges.

Another way to collaborate creatively is to participate in online communities. Whether you're interested in business, marketing, or any other field, there are likely many online communities where you can connect with like-minded individuals and exchange ideas. Participating in these communities can help you to stay up-to-date on the latest trends and opportunities in your field, as well as to find new collaborators and partners.

Collaborating creatively often requires taking risks and being open to new ideas. This means being willing to embrace failure and learn from it. When working with others, it's important to be open and honest about your goals and limitations, and to be willing to listen to and learn from others. By working collaboratively with others, we can often achieve more than we ever could alone, and unlock new levels of creative potential.

CHAPTER 8: CONCLUSION

In today's fast-paced world, embracing change is crucial for achieving success. With technology advancing at an unprecedented rate, those who are resistant to change risk being left behind. The ability to adapt to new technologies and ways of doing things is essential for staying competitive in the modern era.

Furthermore, change often leads to innovation and disruption. Those who are willing to embrace change and think creatively are more likely to come up with new ideas and solutions that can lead to success. Creative thinking allows individuals and businesses to differentiate themselves from their competitors and stand out in the crowded marketplace.

Embracing change also means being open to new opportunities and experiences. The world is constantly changing, and new doors of opportunity are opening all the time. It is up to us to recognise and seize these opportunities to achieve our goals and pave the path for success.

Success in the digital age requires a willingness to embrace change. Whether it be adapting to new technologies, thinking creatively, or seizing new opportunities, those who can successfully navigate change will ultimately be the ones who achieve success in the modern era.

The internet has become a crucial tool in business, providing opportunities for online learning and e-commerce. Social media can be leveraged for personal branding and effective online networking. The rise of artificial intelligence brings both benefits and risks, but can be maximised for success if utilised properly and ethically.

Networking remains a significant factor in building relationships, and can be done effectively through social media and cold emailing. Understanding the psychology behind success and embracing failure as a stepping stone can lead to achieving goals. Balancing work and personal life, maintaining healthy habits, and fostering creativity can greatly enhance productivity and success.

In order to live a successful life in the current era, it is important to embrace change and stay up-to-date with the latest technology and techniques. The possibilities are endless and with the right mindset, anyone can achieve their goals and define their own definition of "riches" beyond financial wealth.

Remember when first starting out in business:
Identify your business idea: Consider your skills, interests, and experience. Identify a product or service that you can offer from home. Research the market demand and competition for your chosen idea.

Create a business plan: Outline your business goals, target market, marketing strategies, financial projections, and operational details. A well-thought-out business plan will guide you throughout the process and help you stay organized.

Determine legal requirements: Check the legal and regulatory requirements for operating a home-based business in your area. This may involve obtaining any necessary licenses or permits. Contact your local government or small business association for guidance.

Set up your workspace: Designate a specific area in your home as your workspace. Ensure it is well-equipped with the necessary tools, equipment, and technology for your business. Create an organized and comfortable environment conducive to productivity.

Establish your online presence: In today's digital age, having an online presence is crucial. Create a professional website and consider using social media platforms to promote your business. Use online marketing strategies to reach your target audience effectively.

Develop a marketing plan: Identify your target audience and develop a marketing strategy to reach them. Consider both online and offline marketing techniques, such as social media advertising, content marketing, networking, and word-of-mouth referrals.

Set up a financial system: Establish a separate business bank account to track your income and expenses. Use accounting software to manage your finances effectively. Consult a financial professional if necessary to ensure compliance with tax regulations.

Obtain necessary resources and support: Determine the resources you'll need to run your business smoothly. This may include equipment, software, suppliers, or professional services. Consider joining relevant industry associations or networking groups for support and guidance.

Start small and test the market: Begin by offering your product or service to a small group of customers. Use their feedback to refine your offering and make necessary adjustments before scaling up. This approach minimizes risks and allows for learning and improvement.

Adapt and grow: Stay adaptable and open to feedback. Continuously evaluate your business, monitor market trends, and make adjustments as needed. Seek opportunities for growth and expansion as you establish your business from home.

Remember, starting a business requires dedication, perseverance, and a willingness to learn. It may take time to achieve success, so stay focused and maintain a positive mindset throughout the journey. Good luck!

AFTERWORD

Please take a look at my wide range of books, including: Ten Businesses to Start from Home, Mastering Household Bills & Finances, Autograph Collecting: A Beginners Guide.

I believe in making knowledge accessible to everyone, which is why all my self help and advice books are priced at just 99p / 99c.

I understand the importance of providing affordable resources to empower individuals and help them achieve their goals.

My philosophy is simple: why should self-help or advice books be sold at exorbitant prices when the primary goal is to offer guidance and support to those who need it?

By keeping my prices low, I ensure that my advice reaches as many people as possible.

I believe that everyone deserves a chance to explore new opportunities and discover their true potential, regardless of their financial circumstances.

So, if you're looking to start a business from the comfort of your home, "Ten Businesses to Start from Home" is the perfect guide for you. With practical tips, actionable strategies, this book will inspire and equip you to embark on your entrepreneurial journey.

Remember, your dreams shouldn't be limited by your budget.

I'm here to provide affordable resources that can make a difference in your life.

Get started today and unlock a world of possibilities!

HELPFUL WEBSITES

Coursera (**www.coursera.org**): Offers a wide range of online courses and specializations from top universities and institutions worldwide. You can audit courses for free or opt for paid certificates.

edX (**www.edx.org**): Similar to Coursera, edX provides access to high-quality online courses from renowned universities, including some in the UK. It offers both free and paid options.

FutureLearn (**www.futurelearn.com**): A UK-based platform offering courses from top universities and cultural institutions. It features both free and paid courses, with the option to earn a certificate upon completion.

LinkedIn Learning (**www.linkedin.com/learning**): Formerly known as Lynda.com, LinkedIn Learning offers a vast library of video courses covering various topics, including business, technology, and creative skills. It requires a subscription.

OpenLearn (**www.open.edu/openlearn**): The Open University's free learning platform provides access to a broad range of courses, materials, and resources across multiple subjects.

Codecademy (**www.codecademy.com**): Focused on coding and programming, Codecademy offers interactive lessons to learn languages like Python, JavaScript, HTML, and more.

Skillshare (**www.skillshare.com**): Skillshare is a platform that offers a wide range of creative courses, including design, photography, writing, and marketing. It operates on a subscription model.

Khan Academy (**www.khanacademy.org**): Khan Academy offers free educational content covering subjects like math, science, humanities, and more. It includes video lessons, practice exercises, and quizzes.

Google Digital Garage (learndigital.withgoogle.com/digitalgarage): Provides free courses and certifications in digital marketing, analytics, and other digital skills. It is a great resource for improving your online presence.

The Open University (**www.open.ac.uk**): As a distance learning institution, The Open University offers a wide range of degree courses, short courses, and online resources across various subjects.

Udemy (**www.udemy.com**): Udemy is a popular online learning marketplace that offers a vast collection of courses on various subjects. It covers everything from business and technology to personal development and creative skills. Courses are created by instructors worldwide, and you can learn at your own pace. Udemy often provides discounts and promotions, making courses affordable. It offers a mix of free and paid courses.

Pluralsight (**www.pluralsight.com**): Pluralsight is an online platform specifically tailored for technology professionals. It provides a vast library of courses and learning paths on programming, cybersecurity, cloud computing, data science, and IT infrastructure. Pluralsight offers both individual and business subscriptions.

Alison (alison.com): Alison is a free online learning platform that offers courses and certifications across various subjects. It provides a mix of self-paced courses and interactive multimedia formats. Alison focuses on practical skills and career development, with courses in areas like business, technology, healthcare, and languages.

Remember to explore the websites to find courses and subjects that align with your interests and learning goals. Each platform has its own unique features and strengths, so it's worth exploring multiple options to find the best fit for you.

Dont forget to check individual websites for course availability, fees (if any), and certification options. These platforms offer a wealth of knowledge and can be excellent resources for enhancing your skills and knowledge in the UK.

www.ingramcontent.com/pod-product-compliance
Lightning Source LLC
Chambersburg PA
CBHW072236230526
45466CB00024B/2053